# Our Senses
# Touch

## Kay Woodward

HODDER
Wayland

an imprint of Hodder Children's Books

Our Senses
Hearing • Sight • Smell • Taste • Touch

For more information on this series and other Hodder Wayland titles,
go to www.hodderwayland.co.uk

## Senses – Touch

Copyright © 2005 Hodder Wayland
First published in 2005 by Hodder Wayland,
an imprint of Hodder Children's Books.

Commissioning Editor: Victoria Brooker       Book Editor: Katie Sergeant
Consultant: Carol Ballard                    Picture Research: Katie Sergeant
Book Designer: Jane Hawkins                  Cover: Hodder Children's Books

British Library Cataloguing in Publication Data
Woodward, Kay
   Touch. - (Our Senses)
   1.Touch - Juvenile literature
   I.Title
   612.8'8

ISBN 0750246731

Printed in China by WKT Company Ltd

Hodder Children's Books
A division of Hodder Headline Limited
338 Euston Road, London NW1 3BH

Cover: You can feel the delicate touch of
a butterfly on your hands.

Picture Acknowledgements
The publisher would like to thank the following for permission to
reproduce their pictures: Corbis 7 (Tom & Dee Ann McCarthy),
*Imprint page* and 10 (Royalty-Free), 12 (Ariel Skelley), 13 (Jutta
Klee), 14 (Michal Heron), 15 (Joe Bator), 20 (Charles Krebs),
21 (Peter Johnson); FLPA 19 (Hugh Clark); Getty Images *Cover*
(Stone/Garry Wade), 4 (Stone/Clarissa Leahy), 5 (The Image
Bank/Don Klumpp), *Title page* and 8 (Thinkstock/Royalty-Free),
11 (The Image Bank/White Packert), 18 (Photodisc Green/Santokh
Kochar/Royalty-Free); Wayland Picture Library 9, 16, 17, 22, 23.
Artwork on page 6 is by Peter Bull.

# Contents

Words in **bold** can be found in the glossary on page 24.

# Touching things

The world is filled with things to touch. There are smooth stones and rough rocks. There are sticky sweets and squashy sofas.

▲ A kitten's coat is smooth and furry.

Our **sense** of touch allows us to **feel** the
amazing things all around. By touching
things, we find out about them. We touch
with our skin.

# How we touch

This shows a section of the skin. There are thousands of nerve endings under the skin. ▼

hair

nerve endings

skin

touch information travels to the brain

There are thousands of **nerve endings** under your skin. When you touch things, these nerve endings send **information** to your brain.

There are lots of nerve endings in your hands, lips, face, neck, tongue and feet. These parts of your body have a good sense of touch. You can feel things best of all with your fingertips.

There are lots of nerve endings in each fingertip. ▼

7

# Rough and smooth

Touching things tells us what they feel like. Different things have different **textures**. The bark of a tree is rough. This page is smooth.

Concrete is hard. Cotton wool is soft
and fluffy. If you hold clay in your hand,
it feels squidgy and wet.

# Hot and cold

When you touch things, you can tell if they are hot or cold. A mug of cocoa warms your fingertips. Try holding someone's hand. This feels warm too!

◄ This mug feels warm.

10

Some things are cold when you touch them. Ice lollies, **icicles**, snowballs and snowmen feel icy cold. A glass filled with a cold drink feels cold to the touch.

An ice lolly feels very cold on your tongue. ▶

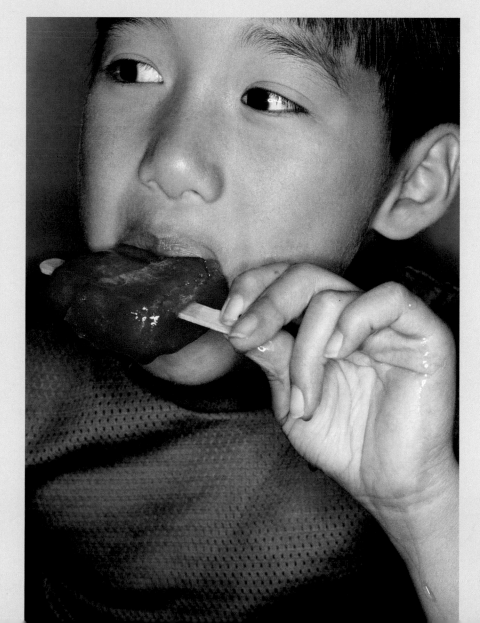

# Ouch!

Some things are dangerous to touch. Very hot things, such as boiling water and fire, can **hurt** you.

▲ Stay well back from the fire.

Very sharp things, such as knives and needles, can give you a nasty cut. Be very careful when you touch them.

Adults will always help with sharp things. ▶

# Seeing by touch

The sense of touch helps people who cannot see. It helps them to feel what things are like in the world around them.

▲ Blind people use their sense of touch to read.

Braille is a special type of writing that can be read with the fingertips. Instead of letters, there are raised dots.

# Touching

You use your sense of touch all day, every day. You touch the buttons on a telephone to make a call. You might touch your hair to push it out of your eyes. You are touching this book right now.

Your sense of touch
tells you when you are
touching something.
Without a sense of
touch, you wouldn't
feel the bench you are
sitting on. You
wouldn't be able
to feel the difference
between a sponge and
a stone.

# Animals

Animals who spend some of their time in dark places use their sense of touch. A cat's whiskers brush against objects. In the dark, this helps it to find its way.

▲ Cats have very long whiskers.

Moles are almost blind. Instead of seeing, they touch things. A mole's nose and whiskers help it to find food.

# Minibeasts

Insects have tiny hairs on their bodies. The smallest breath of air is enough to move the hairs. This sends information to the insect's brain.

Caterpillars have very poor sight. Instead, small hairs all over their bodies tell these creatures about the world all around them.

# What can you feel?

1. Gather together a collection of different objects –
   some squidgy, some hard, some rough, some
   smooth. Put each object in a different box. Without
   looking in the boxes, ask a friend to touch each
   object, one by one. The friend has to try to guess
   what each object is. How many did they get right?

2. Touch different things,
   such as some wet clay,
   a wobbly jelly, the bark of a tree, a pillow,
   an ice cube, a piece of velvet or a knitted
   jumper. Can you describe what each
   feels like?

3. Take two pencils. Ask a friend to shut
   their eyes. Now lightly touch the two
   pencils on to their fingertip. How many
   things does your friend feel? Now do the
   same on their leg. Does your friend still
   feel two things?

   There are many more nerve endings on
   your fingertips. This is why it is much
   easier to feel things here than it
   is on your leg or other
   parts of your body.

# Glossary

**feel**         To touch something to find out what it is like.

**hurt**         When someone feels pain.

**icicle**        A thin, pointed piece of ice that hangs down.

**information**    Things that tell you about something.

**nerve ending**  Part of your body that sends messages to the brain.

**sense**        The power to see, hear, smell, feel or taste.

**texture**      What the surface of something feels like, for example, rough or smooth.

# Index